FRANCHISING IN EGYPT 2014

Legal and Business Considerations

Kendal H. Tyre, Jr., Executive Editor
Diana Vilmenay-Hammond, Managing Editor
Courtney L. Lindsay, II, Assistant Editor

LexNoir Foundation

First Quarter 2014

LexNoir Foundation is the charitable, educational arm of LexNoir, an international network of lawyers connecting the African Diaspora.

This publication, *Franchising in Egypt 2014: Legal and Business Considerations*, contains excerpts from *Franchising in Africa 2014: Legal and Business Considerations*. Both works are published by LexNoir Foundation and reflect the points of view of the authors and editors as of the date of publication and do not necessarily represent the opinions, interpretations, or positions of the law firms or organizations with which they are affiliated, nor the opinions, interpretations or positions of LexNoir Foundation or LexNoir.

Nothing contained in this book is to be considered as the rendering of legal advice, either generally or in connection with any specific issues or case. Readers are responsible for obtaining advice from their own legal counsel or other professional. This book, any forms and agreements or other information herein are intended for educational and informational purposes only.

www.lexnoir.org

Table of Contents

Franchising in Egypt

Girgis Abd El-Shahid
Sarwat A. Shahid Law Firm

Bibliography of International Franchise Resources

Kendal H. Tyre, Jr., Diana Vilmenay-Hammond, Pierce Haesung Han, Courtney L. Lindsay, II and Keri McWilliams
Nixon Peabody LLP

Acknowledgment

This book could not have been written without the hard work and dedication of each of the contributing authors and editors. Thank you.

We would like to acknowledge and extend our heartfelt gratitude to Michael Collier and Maria Stallings of the Washington, D.C. office of Nixon Peabody LLP for their invaluable assistance in revising, proofing, and editing this publication.

About the Editors and Authors

Kendal H. Tyre, Jr. – Kendal is a partner in the Washington, D.C. office of Nixon Peabody LLP. He handles domestic and cross-border transactions, including mergers and acquisitions, joint ventures, strategic alliances, licensing, and franchise matters.

In his franchise and licensing practice, Kendal counsels domestic and international franchisors, franchisees, licensors, licensees and distributors regarding U.S. state and federal franchise laws as well as foreign franchise legislation in a variety of jurisdictions. Kendal drafts and provides advice with regard to franchise and license agreements, disclosure documents and area development agreements and has extensive experience drafting and negotiating a variety of other commercial agreements. His client base spans the United States and foreign countries, including South Africa, Kenya, and the United Kingdom.

Kendal is a frequent contributor to franchise publications and a frequent speaker at franchise programs held by the American Bar Association Forum on Franchising and the International Franchise Association.

Kendal is co-chair of the firm's Diversity Action Committee and its Africa Group. Kendal is also the executive director of LexNoir Foundation.

E-mail address: ktyre@nixonpeabody.com

Diana Vilmenay-Hammond – Diana is an attorney in the Washington, D.C. office of Nixon Peabody LLP. She is a member of the firm's Franchise & Distribution Team.

In her franchise practice, Diana works with domestic and international franchisors on transactional and litigation matters. Specifically, she counsels franchisor clients regarding state and federal franchise laws, disclosure and registration obligations.

Diana drafts and negotiates various commercial agreements, including international franchise and development agreements.

Diana has co-authored numerous articles on franchising and frequently co-hosted the Nixon Peabody franchise law webinar series. Topics have included:

- "Franchise Case Law Round-Up: Implications for Your Franchise," February 15, 2012;
- "Social Media Part II: Best Practices in Protecting Your Brand in the New Media," September 14, 2010; and
- "The Awuah Case: Bellwether or Outlier," May 11, 2010

Diana received her J.D. from Howard University School of Law and her B.A. from Georgetown University. She is a member of the American Bar Association (Forum on Franchising).

Email address: dvilmenay@nixonpeabody.com

Pierce Haesung Han – Pierce is an associate in Nixon Peabody's Global Business & Transactions Group. Pierce focuses his practice on three main areas, assisting clients with a variety of complex business transactions.

- Mergers & Acquisitions: Providing assistance to both public and private clients with various mergers and acquisitions, performing due diligence, drafting and negotiating transaction documents, and facilitating closing and post-closing mechanics.
- International Commercial Transactions: Drafting and negotiating a variety of commercial agreements, including international franchise and development agreements, license agreements, and purchase and sale agreements.
- Federal Securities Law Matters: Assisting public and private clients regarding federal securities laws and stock exchange rules relating to corporate governance and disclosure.

Pierce serves as the Secretary of the Asian Pacific Bar Association Educational Fund (an affiliate of the Asian Pacific American Bar Association of the Greater Washington, D.C. Area).

Pierce received his J.D. from Georgetown University Law Center and his B.A. from Case Western Reserve University. He is admitted to practice in the State of New York and the District of Columbia.

E-mail address: phan@nixonpeabody.com

Courtney L. Lindsay, II – Courtney is an associate in Nixon Peabody's Corporate and Finance practice. In his corporate practice, Courtney assists for-profit and non-profit entities with transactional matters and corporate governance. In various capacities, Courtney has been involved in multiple merger and acquisition transactions, including drafting and managing due diligence.

Previously, Courtney worked in the legal and business affairs department at a national cable network, where he handled matters related to the network's LLC agreement, including drafting board and member consent agreements.

Courtney received his J.D. from the University of Virginia School of Law and his B.A. from the University of Virginia. He is admitted to practice in the Commonwealth of Virginia and the District of Columbia.

E-mail address: clindsay@nixonpeabody.com

Keri McWilliams – Keri is an associate in the Franchise & Distribution team of Nixon Peabody LLP. Keri works with clients on a number of franchising issues, including obtaining and maintaining franchise registrations in various states, responding to state inquiries regarding trade practices, ongoing compliance with state and federal regulations, and updating franchise disclosure documents. She also handles franchise sales counseling and franchise system issues.

Keri is a member of the American Bar Association's Forum on Franchising, and the Federal and Minnesota State bar associations. She is also a member of Minnesota Women Lawyers and the Minnesota Association of Black Lawyers, and a volunteer in the Volunteer Lawyers Network.

Keri received her J.D. from the Georgetown University Law Center and her B.F.A. from Washington University. She is admitted to practice in the District of Columbia and Minnesota.

E-mail address: kmcwilliams@nixonpeabody.com

Girgis Abd El-Shahid – Girgis is an attorney in the Sarwat A. Shahid Law Firm in Cairo, Egypt. He is a former Public Prosecutor. He received an LL.M. in International Legal Studies from Georgetown University Law Center, U.S.A., an LL.B. from Cairo University, English Section, and a B.A. in Economics and Minor in Business Administration from the American University in Cairo. Since his entry into the private practice of law, Girgis has provided legal services to numerous national and multinational companies operating in the Middle East Region. He specializes in banking and finance, securities offerings, joint venture arrangements, acquisitions, legal due diligence, corporate and commercial agreements, telecommunications, and intellectual property litigation. Girgis speaks Arabic and English.

E-mail address: girgis.shahid@shahidlaw.com

About the Book

Franchising in Egypt 2014: Legal and Business Considerations contains excerpts from the larger work, *Franchising in Africa 2014: Legal and Business Considerations*. Both books serve as practical, succinct, easy-to-use reference tools for lawyers, business people and academics to use in navigating the myriad laws and business issues impacting franchise arrangements on the African continent.

This book provides an overview of the franchise industry in Egypt and addresses the typical legal issues confronted when expanding a franchise system in Egypt. The larger work, *Franchising in Africa 2014: Legal and Business Considerations*, covers those laws governing franchising in fifteen other African countries – Angola, Botswana, Burundi, Cape Verde, Democratic Republic of Congo, Ethiopia, Ghana, Kenya, Mozambique, Nigeria, Rwanda, South Africa, Tunisia, Zambia and Zimbabwe.

In both books, an author, who is a legal expert in the designated jurisdiction, addresses the basic questions that a franchise lawyer would need to know to competently represent a client in expanding their franchise system to that country.

Each country chapter organizes a discussion of that country's laws under various headings and in a uniform format. Topics were sent to each country's author in the form of a questionnaire, and each author drafted responses to the questions presented. A general overview relating to the political and economic history of the country at the beginning of each chapter provides an initial context for the regulatory framework. [1]

---

[1] The source of information for these sections is the Central Intelligence Agency, https://www.cia.gov/library/publications/the-world-factbook/ (last visited November 3, 2013).

Apart from an overview of the legal framework for franchising, each book contains other articles and resources that should prove useful to those in the franchise industry.

The authors for each chapter are listed at the beginning of a chapter and their biographical information is listed in the previous section, *About the Editors and Authors*.

Readers should always consult with local counsel in the relevant jurisdiction instead of relying solely on the information contained in this book. The laws governing franchising are evolving and local counsel in Egypt are best positioned to provide timely, relevant advice applying the current law to the particular facts of a case.

Franchising in Egypt

Girgis Abd El-Shahid

Sarwat A. Shahid Law Firm

Cairo, Egypt

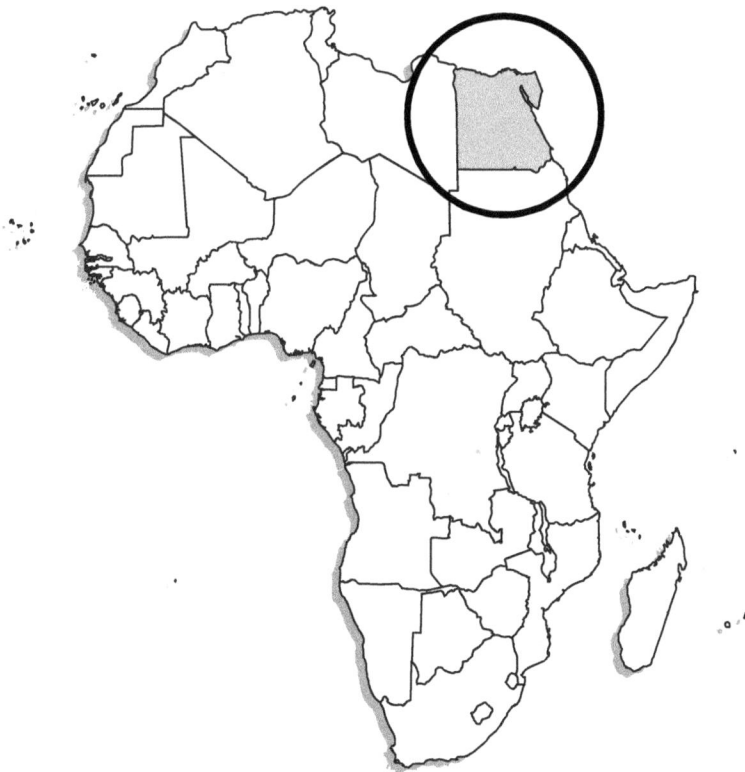

Egypt

I.   Introduction

A.   Historical Background of Country

Partially independent from the United Kingdom in 1922, Egypt acquired full sovereignty with the overthrow of the British-backed monarchy in 1952. The completion of the Aswan High Dam in 1971 and the resultant Lake Nasser have altered the time-honored place of the Nile River in the agriculture and ecology of Egypt. A rapidly growing population, limited arable land, and dependence on the Nile all continue to overtax resources and stress society. The government has struggled to meet the demands of Egypt's population through economic reform and massive investment in communications and physical infrastructure. Inspired by the 2010 Tunisian revolution, Egyptian opposition groups led demonstrations and labor strikes countrywide, culminating in President Hosni Mubarak's ouster. Egypt's military assumed national leadership until a new parliament was in place in early 2012. The same year candidate, Mohammed Mursi, won the presidential election and a new constitution was affirmed. In July 2013, the military ousted Mursi and he was replaced by interim president Adly Mansour.

B.   Economy of the Country

Occupying the northeast corner of the African continent, Egypt is bisected by the highly fertile Nile valley, where most economic activity takes place. Egypt's economy was highly centralized during the rule of former President Gamal Abdel Nasser but opened up considerably under former Presidents Anwar El-Sadat and Mohamed Hosni Mubarak. Cairo from 2004 to 2008 aggressively pursued economic reforms to attract foreign investment and facilitate GDP growth; however, the global financial crisis slowed reform efforts. In 2010, the government spent more on infrastructure and public projects, and exports drove GDP growth to more than 5%.

After unrest erupted in January 2011, the Egyptian government backtracked on economic reforms, drastically increasing social spending to address public dissatisfaction but political uncertainty at the same time caused economic growth to slow significantly, reducing the government's revenues. Tourism, manufacturing and construction were among the hardest hit sectors of the Egyptian economy and economic growth is likely to remain slow during the next several years.

C.   Franchise Legal Overview

The *Egyptian Civil Code of 1948* (the "Civil Code") and *Commercial Code of 1999 (Law No. 17)* (the "Commercial Code") govern commercial activities in Egypt since there are no specific laws regarding franchising and distribution in the country. Consequently, the rights and obligations of parties to a franchise agreement will be construed according to the provisions of Egypt's general commercial laws which are the main sources of legal rules regarding contracts. A franchise agreement may, however, be governed by the Commercial Code, if it is construed as a transfer of technology.

II.   Regulatory Requirements

A.   Pre-Sale Disclosure

Please describe any pre-sale franchise disclosure or similar requirements that may apply to franchise transactions.

No pre-sale franchise disclosure or similar requirements apply to franchise transactions under the laws of Egypt.

B.   Governmental Approvals, Registrations, Filing Requirements

Please describe any necessary government approvals, registrations, or filing requirements that may apply to franchise transactions.

There are no government approvals, registrations, or filing requirements that apply to franchise transactions.

Egypt

See, however, Section V (Trademarks) of this chapter relating to the registration of trademark licenses under the *Egyptian Intellectual Property Rights Law.*

C. Limits of Fees and Typical Term of Franchise Agreement

Please describe any limits upon the nature and extent of fees and the term of a typical franchise agreement.

There are no set provisions related to the nature and extent of fees and the term of a franchise agreement.

III. Currency

If all payments under a franchise agreement must be made in immediately available U.S. Dollars, please advise as to any restrictions, reporting requirements, or regulations concerning the exchange, repatriation, or remittance of U.S. Dollars.

Previously, there were no restrictions, reporting requirements, or regulations concerning the exchange, repatriation, or remittance of U.S. Dollars imposed by the Central Bank of Egypt or any other competent authority of the Arab Republic of Egypt, except that currency transfers must be made through a local bank or an institution permitted to deal with foreign currencies.[2] Since the events that took place in Egypt in January 201,1 the Central Bank of Egypt has set certain rules limiting and/or regulating persons' ability to transfer foreign funds outside of Egypt.

---

[2] *See The Banking Sector and the Money Law No. 88* for the year 2003 and its Executive Regulations. According to Article 5 of the *Treaty between the United States of America and the Arab Republic of Egypt concerning the Reciprocal Encouragement and Protection of Investments,* Egypt and the United States shall grant the "free transfer of ... royalties and other payments deriving from licenses, franchises and other similar grants of rights."

Egypt

IV.   Taxes, Tariffs, and Duties

Please do not provide any in-depth comments on tax structuring. However, please provide your general comments on the typical amount of withholding tax that would apply and whether a "gross-up" provision contained in a franchise agreement would be enforceable in your country.

The Egyptian Tax Law stipulates that payments of service fees or royalties made to non-residents of Egypt are subject to a 20% withholding tax.

A "gross up" provision contained in a franchise agreement would be enforceable in Egypt.

Egypt has entered into double taxation treaties with a number of countries, including the United States.[3]

V.   Trademarks

Please advise us as to whether there are any special requirements for granting a valid trademark license, including the use of a registered user agreement or a short trademark license agreement and any required filing of such an agreement with the trademark authorities.

In strict compliance with the *Egyptian Intellectual Property Rights Law* ("IPR Law"), trademark licenses should be registered at the Trademark Office to make them enforceable vis-à-vis third parties. The trademark license, whether taking a form of a normal trademark license agreement, or a registered user

---

[3]   Egypt has double taxation treaties with: Albania, Algeria, Austria, Bahrain, Belarus, Belgium, Bulgaria, Canada, China, Cyprus, Czech Republic, Denmark, Finland, France, Germany, Greece, Holland, Hungary, India, Indonesia, Iraq, Italy, Japan, Jordan, Kuwait, Lebanon, Libya, Malaysia, Malta, Montenegro, Morocco, North Korea, Norway, Pakistan, Palestine, Poland, Romania, Russia, Serbia, Singapore, South Africa, Spain, Sudan, Sweden, Switzerland, Syria, Tunisia, Turkey, Ukraine, United Arab Emirates, United Kingdom, United States, and Yemen.

agreement, must be duly notarized, consularized, and legalized by the appropriate Egyptian consulate.

Notwithstanding any registration requirements under the IPR Law, it is highly recommended that parties not register any trademark license agreements for the following reasons:

- The Trademark Office takes a very passive attitude when requested to deregister any license, especially in case of a dispute between the parties;

- The second paragraph of Article 95 of the IPR Law stipulates that the "mark owner may only terminate or choose not to renew [a] license based on a legitimate reason." It is not clear whether the lapse or expiration of the term of an agreement is deemed to be legitimate. Local practitioners are contesting the constitutionality of this clause in the hope of striking it from the IPR Law; and

- The lack of registration does not affect the enforceability of any agreement between the parties.

VI.   Restrictions on Transfer

Please advise as to whether there are any restrictions (1) on a franchisor to restrict transfers by a master franchisee, any interest in a master franchisee, or the assets of the master franchisee or (2) the ability of a master franchisee to control and/or restrict transfers of a subfranchisee's rights under a master franchise agreement, interest in the subfranchisee, or the assets of the subfranchisee.

There are no definite transfer restrictions on a franchisor towards the master franchisee as it depends on the franchise transaction. Further, the master franchisee can impose reciprocal transfer restrictions on the subfranchisees.

VII. Termination

Please advise us as to any laws relating to termination in your country, such as agency laws, required indemnity provisions, notice or "good cause" requirements, or other laws affecting termination of a franchise agreement. Please describe.

The Egyptian law allows parties to terminate a franchise agreement, provided one of the parties commits an act of breach and such defaulting party is obliged to indemnify the non-defaulting party for the loss suffered as a result for such termination. Further, the law allows the contracting parties to fix in advance the amount of damages in the franchise agreement to be paid in the event of a contractual breach.[4]

VIII. Governing Law, Jurisdiction, and Dispute Resolution

A. Choice of Law of Foreign Jurisdiction

Please confirm whether the choice of law of a foreign jurisdiction would likely to be upheld under the law of the country, except for certain matters such as trademarks, bankruptcy, and competition matters, which we assume would be governed by the law in your country.

---

[4]   *Editor's note:* Egyptian practitioners are divided on whether the *Commercial Agency Law* (*Law No. 120 of 1982*) applies to the franchisor-franchisee relationship. This law regulates the licensing and operation of commercial agents. If this law were applied to franchise arrangements, the application of local law would be mandatory with respect to: (1) notice and opportunity to cure prior to termination, (2) notice prior to non-renewal and (3) compensation for breaches. It is difficult to predict how a judge in Egypt may interpret the compensation requirement, because there is no compensation formula in the law. Regardless, providing for waivers of agency law rights in the franchise agreement is advisable. *See* Mazero and Maisonneuve, *supra* note 90, at 15. Recently, the Egyptian Constitutional Court rendered a provision allowing for compensation in case of the non-renewal of a fixed term agency null and void.

In the event that a franchise agreement is construed as a "transfer of technology" agreement under the Commercial Code, then it will be mandatorily subject to Egyptian law.

The Commercial Code does not contain a definition of "technology" and the Egyptian Court of Cassation (the Supreme Court Equivalent in Egypt) has not yet issued any judgments further interpreting its provisions. Most local practitioners are of the opinion that a technology transfer was meant to capture franchise arrangements. Other practitioners are of the opinion that franchise arrangements are only deemed to be captured by technology transfer if a great deal of "know-how" is transferred from the franchisor to the franchisee.

If a franchise agreement is not construed as a "transfer of technology" agreement, the parties may choose the governing law, and their choice will be upheld under Egyptian law. Egyptian law recognizes the choice of the parties, except for those provisions conflicting with Egyptian public policy.

B.   International Arbitration Dispute Resolution

Please confirm that a court in your country would honor an election of international arbitration dispute resolution, and therefore refuse to hear any disputes arising under a franchise agreement.

Egypt is a signatory to the *Convention on the Recognition and Enforcement of Foreign Arbitral Awards* (the "New York Convention"). Therefore, an arbitral award under international rules, such as the *ICC Rules of Conciliation and Arbitration* or the like would be recognized and enforced by the Egyptian courts without re-examination of the merits.

In order to enforce a foreign arbitral award in Egypt, the award must first be deposited with a special expert office at the Ministry of Justice. This expert office then determines whether to accept such deposit based on certain thresholds, mainly related to whether such award infringes any Egyptian public policy or mandatory rules. Once the award is deposited at this expert office, the depositor may file a case before the Courts of Appeal for execution.

If the franchise agreement is construed as a "transfer of technology" agreement under the Commercial Code, the venue of arbitration must be in Egypt. Otherwise, the venue will be honored by an Egyptian court.

IX.   Non-Competition Provisions

If the franchise agreement prohibits the master franchisee from engaging in certain competitive activities during the term of the agreement, and for a 12-month period after the termination or expiration of the agreement, please comment on the enforceability of non-competition covenants in your country.

The Egyptian law respects the importance of the protection of the know-how. Accordingly, it allows the parties to any agreement to protect it in the way they deem appropriate.

If the franchise arrangement is deemed to be captured by the notion of technology transfer, Egyptian law restricts the technology provider from imposing any condition in the technology transfer contract, which restricts the freedom of the transferee in using the technology. The foregoing, however, shall not apply if these conditions are provided in the technology transfer contract for the protection of consumers or for safeguarding a legitimate interest of the supplier of technology.

Egyptian jurisprudence does not provide clear guidance as to what can be deemed to be a "legitimate interest of the supplier of technology."

X.   Language Requirements

Does the law in your country require that a franchise agreement be translated into the local language in order to be enforceable between the parties?

There is no requirement that a franchise agreement be translated into local language in order to be enforceable between the parties.

XI.   Other Significant Matters

Please advise as to whether there are any significant matters not addressed above of which a franchisor should be aware in connection with its entering into a franchise agreement in your country.

Depending on the magnitude of the know-how transferred, a franchise agreement may or may not be construed as an agreement involving a "transfer of technology" and thereby subjecting the agreement to specific rules stipulated in the Egyptian Commercial Code, which in spirit favors the franchisee.[5]

---

[5]   *Editor's note*: Certain practitioners in Egypt believe that franchise agreements would be subject to the provisions of the Commercial Code (*Law No. 17 of 1999*) governing transfer of technology agreements (the "Technology Transfer Provisions"). If so, as previously noted, the agreements would be subject to mandatory Egyptian choice-of-law and choice-of-forum provisions. It might also be more difficult for a franchisor to terminate the agreements pursuant to their terms. The Technology Transfer Provisions may not apply to franchise agreements because the Commercial Code exempts franchise agreements authorizing the use of trademarks or trade names, unless such use includes a transfer of "technical data." Most franchise agreements would not likely contemplate such a transfer. Disclaimers that the Technology Transfer Provisions do not apply have not been tested in Egyptian courts. As a result, they are of uncertain enforceability in Egypt. However, an express disclaimer of the Technology Transfer Provisions would still mitigate the risk that a foreign court or arbitral tribunal might itself determine that the mandatory choice-of-forum provisions in the Technology Transfer Provisions would deprive it of

Egypt

Bibliography of International Franchise Resources

Kendal H. Tyre, Jr., Diana Vilmenay-Hammond, Pierce Haesung Han, Courtney L. Lindsay, II, and Keri McWilliams

Nixon Peabody LLP

Washington, D.C.

I. General International Resources

Mark Abell, Gary R. Duvall, and Andrea Oricchio Kirsh, *International Franchise Legislation* B1, ABA FORUM ON FRANCHISING (1996)

Kathleen C. Anderson and Anthony M. Stiegler, *Put Muscle in Your Marks: Enforcing Intellectual Property Rights* W14, ABA FORUM ON FRANCHISING (1995)

Richard M. Asbill and Jane W. LaFranchi, *International Franchise Sales Laws—A Survey* W7, ABA FORUM ON FRANCHISING (2005)

Jeffery A. Brimer, Alison C. McElroy, and John Pratt, *Going International: What Additional Restraints Will You Face?* W4, ABA FORUM ON FRANCHISING (2011)

Michael G. Brennan, Alexander Konigsberg, and Philip F. Zeidman, *Globetrotting: A Workshop on International Franchising* 10/W8, ABA FORUM ON FRANCHISING (1994)

Michael G. Brennan, Alexander Konigsberg, and Philip F. Zeidman, *Globetrotting: Strategies for Launching U.S. Franchisors Abroad* 2/P2, ABA FORUM ON FRANCHISING (1994)

Christopher P. Bussert and Jennifer Dolman, *Regaining Your Trademark After Abandonment or Misappropriation* W7, ABA FORUM ON FRANCHISING (2011)

Ronald T. Coleman and Linda K. Stevens, *Trade Secrets and Confidential Information: Rights and Remedies* W2, ABA FORUM ON FRANCHISING (2000)

Finola Cunningham, *Commerce Department Helps Franchisors Go Global*, in FRANCHISING WORLD 63 (Dec. 2005)

Michael R. Daigle and Alex S. Konigsberg, *Meeting Off-Shore Disclosure and Contract Requirements* F/W13, ABA FORUM ON FRANCHISING (1992)

Jennifer Dolman, Robert A. Lauer, and Lawrence M. Weinberg, *Structuring International Master Franchise Relationships for Success and Responding When Things Go Awry* W22, ABA FORUM ON FRANCHISING (2007)

Gary R. Duvall, Paul Jones, and Jane LaFranchi, *Planning for the International Enforcement of Franchise Agreements* W6, ABA FORUM ON FRANCHISING (1999)

William Edwards, *International Expansion: Do Opportunities Outweigh Challenges?* in FRANCHISING WORLD (February 2008)

George J. Eydt and Stuart Hershman, *Bringing a Foreign Franchise System to the United States* W9, ABA FORUM ON FRANCHISING (2009)

William A. Finkelstein and Louis T. Pirkey, *International Trademarks* W15, ABA FORUM ON FRANCHISING (1991)

William A. Finkelstein, *Protecting Trademarks Internationally: Current Strategies and Developments* B3, ABA FORUM ON FRANCHISING (1996)

Stephen Giles, Lou H. Jones, and Lawrence Weinberg, *Negotiating and Documenting Complex International Franchise Agreements* W21, ABA FORUM ON FRANCHISING (2006)

Steven M. Goldman, Stephen Giles, Marc Israel, and Stanley Wong, *Competition Round Up from Around the World* LB2, ABA FORUM ON FRANCHISING (2004)

David C. Gryce and E. Lynn Perry, *Trademarks and Copyrights in the International Arena* 6/W4, ABA FORUM ON FRANCHISING (1993)

Kenneth S. Kaplan, Andrew P. Loewinger, and Penelope J. Ward, *System Standards in International Franchising* W14, ABA FORUM ON FRANCHISING (2005)

Edward Levitt and Jorge Mondragon, *A Survey of International Legal Traps and How to Avoid Them—Beyond the Franchise Laws* W20, ABA FORUM ON FRANCHISING (2007)

Ned Levitt, Kendal H. Tyre, and Penny Ward, *The Impossible Dream: Controlling Your International Franchise System* W4, ABA FORUM ON FRANCHISING (2010)

Michael K. Lindsey and Andrew P. Loewinger, *International (Non-U.S.) Franchise Disclosure Requirements* W9, ABA FORUM ON FRANCHISING (2002)

Andrew P. Loewinger and John Pratt, *Recent Changes and Trends in International Franchise Laws* W4, ABA FORUM ON FRANCHISING (2008)

Andrew P. Loewinger and Thomas M. Pitegoff, *Avoiding the Long Arm of the Law in International Franchising: Issues and Approaches* W8, ABA FORUM ON FRANCHISING (1995)

Craig J. Madson and Katherine C. Spelman, *Similarity and Confusion in the Intellectual Property Arena* W11, ABA FORUM ON FRANCHISING (1997)

Christopher A. Nowak, John Pratt, and Carl E. Zwisler, *Franchising Internationally with Countries with Opaque Legal Systems* W20, ABA FORUM ON FRANCHISING (2006)

E. Lynn Perry and John L. Sullivan Jr., *Trademark Compliance and Enforcement Techniques* E/W12, ABA FORUM ON FRANCHISING (1992)

Marcel Portmann, *Franchising Sector Proves Global Reach*, in FRANCHISING WORLD (January 2007)

John Pratt and Luiz Henrique O. do Amaral, *Civil Law for Common Law Practitioners (or How to Draft an Agreement for Use Overseas)* W4, ABA FORUM ON FRANCHISING (2002)

Kirk W. Reilly, Robert F. Salkowski and Geoffrey B. Shaw, *Determining the Rules of Engagement in Litigation Here and Abroad* W5, ABA FORUM ON FRANCHISING (2008)

Catherine Riesterer and Frank Zaid, *Basics of International Franchising* L/B2, ABA FORUM ON FRANCHISING (1997)

W. Andrew Scott and Christopher N. Wormald, *Stranger in a Strange Land: Contrasting Franchising in International Expansion* W2, ABA FORUM ON FRANCHISING (2003)

Donald Smith and Erik Wulff, *International Franchising: The Unraveling of an International Franchise Relationship* 15/W13, ABA FORUM ON FRANCHISING (1993)

Frank Zaid, Pamela Mills, and Michael Santa Maria, *Essential Issues in International Franchising* LB/1, ABA FORUM ON FRANCHISING (2001)

II. African Resources

Joyce G. Mazero and J. Perry Maisonneuve, *Franchising in the Middle East and North Africa* W2, ABA FORUM ON FRANCHISING (2009)

Kendal H. Tyre, Jr. and Diana Vilmenay-Hammond, *Franchise World: A Burgeoning Middle Class Spurs Franchise Investment in Africa*, MINORITY BUSINESS ENTREPRENEUR (November 2012)

Kendal H. Tyre, Jr., *IP Protection May Promote Additional Franchise Growth in Africa*, NIXON PEABODY LLP: FRANCHISING BUSINESS & LAW ALERT (September 2012)

Kendal H. Tyre, Jr., *Market Potential for Franchising in Africa*, NIXON PEABODY LLP: FRANCHISING BUSINESS & LAW ALERT (June 2011)

Kendal H. Tyre, Jr. and Courtney L. Lindsay, II, *Continued Growth of Franchising in Africa*, NIXON PEABODY LLP: FRANCHISE LAW ALERT (April 2013)

Kendal H. Tyre, Jr. and Courtney L. Lindsay, II, *Pan African Franchise Federation Holds Inaugural Meeting*, NIXON PEABODY LLP: AFRICA ALERT (June 2013)

Kendal H. Tyre, Jr. and Courtney L. Lindsay, II, *White House Encouraging Private Investment and Transparency in Sub-Saharan Africa*, NIXON PEABODY LLP: AFRICA ALERT (August 2012)

Kendal H. Tyre, Jr. and Diana Vilmenay-Hammond, *African Economic Growth Impacts Franchising on the Continent*, NIXON PEABODY LLP: FRANCHISE LAW ALERT (July 2012)

Kendal H. Tyre, Jr. and Diana Vilmenay-Hammond, *Franchising in Africa*, in FRANCHISING WORLD (August 2013)

John Sotos and Sam Hall, *African Franchising: Cross-Continent Momentum*, in FRANCHISING WORLD (June 2007)

A.   Angola

João Afonso Fialho, *Franchising in Angola*, in FRANCHISING IN AFRICA: LEGAL AND BUSINESS CONSIDERATIONS 91-105 (Kendal H. Tyre, Jr. & Diana Vilmenay-Hammond eds. 2012)

B.   Botswana

Bonzo Makgalemele, *Franchising in Botswana*, in FRANCHISING IN AFRICA: LEGAL AND BUSINESS CONSIDERATIONS 107-117 (Kendal H. Tyre, Jr. & Diana Vilmenay-Hammond eds. 2012)

C.   Cape Verde

João Afonso Fialho, *Franchising in Cape Verde*, in FRANCHISING IN AFRICA: LEGAL AND BUSINESS CONSIDERATIONS 119-132 (Kendal H. Tyre, Jr. & Diana Vilmenay-Hammond eds. 2012)

D.   Egypt

Girgis Abd El-Shahid, *Franchising in Eqypt*, in FRANCHISING IN AFRICA: LEGAL AND BUSINESS CONSIDERATIONS 133-142 (Kendal H. Tyre, Jr. & Diana Vilmenay-Hammond eds. 2012)

A. Safaa El Din El Oteifi, *Egypt*, in INTERNATIONAL FRANCHISING EGY/1 (Dennis Campbell gen. ed. 2011)

E.   Ethiopia

Yohannes Assefa and Biset Beyene Molla, *Franchising in Ethiopia*, in FRANCHISING IN AFRICA: LEGAL AND BUSINESS CONSIDERATIONS 143-157 (Kendal H. Tyre, Jr. & Diana Vilmenay-Hammond eds. 2012)

Kendal H. Tyre, Jr., Yohannes Assefa and Getachew Mengistie Alemu, *New Intellectual Property Regulation Requires Scramble to Protect Marks in Ethiopia*, NIXON PEABODY LLP: AFRICA ALERT (October 2013)

F.   Ghana

Divine K.D. Letsa and Hawa Tejansie Ajei, *Franchising in Ghana*, in FRANCHISING IN AFRICA: LEGAL AND BUSINESS CONSIDERATIONS 159-167 (Kendal H. Tyre, Jr. & Diana Vilmenay-Hammond eds. 2012)

G.   Libya

Kendal H. Tyre, Jr. & Diana Vilmenay-Hammond, *First U.S. Franchise Opens in Libya*, NIXON PEABODY LLP: AFRICA ALERT (August 2012)

H.   Mozambique

Diogo Xavier da Cunha, *Franchising in Mozambique*, in FRANCHISING IN AFRICA: LEGAL AND BUSINESS CONSIDERATIONS 169-182 (Kendal H. Tyre, Jr. & Diana Vilmenay-Hammond eds. 2012)

I.   Nigeria

Theo Emuwa and Bimbola Fowler-Ekar, *Franchising in Nigeria*, in FRANCHISING IN AFRICA: LEGAL AND BUSINESS CONSIDERATIONS 183-198 (Kendal H. Tyre, Jr. & Diana Vilmenay-Hammond eds. 2012)

Kendal H. Tyre, Jr. and Theo Emuwa, *Nigerian Franchising: Making Your Way Through the Thicket*, NIXON PEABODY LLP: FRANCHISE LAW ALERT (June 2005)

J.   South Africa

Eugene Honey, *Franchising and the New Consumer Protection Bill*, BOWMAN GILFILLAN (March 2008)

Eugene Honey, *Franchising and the Consumer Protection Bill*, BOWMAN GILFILLAN (May 2008)

Eugene Honey, *Pitfalls and Difficulties with the CPA*, ADAMS & ADAMS (March 2013)

Eugene Honey, *Disclosure is Compulsory*, ADAMS & ADAMS (May 2013)

Eugene Honey and Wim Alberts, *Fundamental Consumer Rights: The Right to Equality*, BOWMAN GILFILLAN (March 2009)

Eugene Honey and Wim Alberts, *The Reach of the Consumer Protection Bill: The Final*, BOWMAN GILFILLAN (March 2009)

Eugene Honey, *South Africa*, in GETTING THE DEAL THROUGH: FRANCHISE (2013) 172-178 (Philip F. Zeidman ed. 2013)

Taswell Papier, *Franchising in South Africa*, in FRANCHISING IN AFRICA: LEGAL AND BUSINESS CONSIDERATIONS 199-224 (Kendal H. Tyre, Jr. & Diana Vilmenay-Hammond eds. 2012)

Kendal H. Tyre, Jr., *A New Legal Landscape for Franchising in South Africa*, NIXON PEABODY LLP: FRANCHISING BUSINESS & LAW ALERT (September 2009)

K.   Tunisia

Yessine Ferah, *Franchising in Tunisia*, in FRANCHISING IN AFRICA: LEGAL AND BUSINESS CONSIDERATIONS 225-245 (Kendal H. Tyre, Jr. & Diana Vilmenay-Hammond eds. 2012)

Kendal H. Tyre, Jr., Diana Vilmenay-Hammond, and Yessine Ferah, *New Franchise Legislation in Tunisia*, NIXON PEABODY LLP: FRANCHISE LAW ALERT (September 2010)

L.   Zambia

Mabvuto Sakala, *Franchising in Zambia*, in FRANCHISING IN AFRICA: LEGAL AND BUSINESS CONSIDERATIONS 247-255 (Kendal H. Tyre, Jr. & Diana Vilmenay-Hammond eds. 2012)

www.ingramcontent.com/pod-product-compliance
Lightning Source LLC
Chambersburg PA
CBHW052125230326
41598CB00080B/4429